Leaders Eat Last

Why Some Teams Pull Together and Others Don't

by: Simon Sinek

The Mindset Warrior Summary Guide

D1407614

The
Mindset
Warrior

Table of Contents

Hi there! Be Sure to Stick Around to the End for a FREE BONUS.

My gift to you; as a special thank you for purchasing this book.

-The Mindset Warrior

MW Summary Guide Disclaimer

Introduction

In this Mindset Warrior Summary Guide we cover the main topics discussed in "Leaders Eat Last". This book is intended to supplement your reading and be an easy reference guide. You are encouraged to purchase the original book if you have not already.

The difference between this guide and the actual book, is that we don't go into the lengthy stories and repetition that most books often do. Instead, we share each principle, explain its reasoning, and we provide advice on how you can apply each to your own company culture.

As I always say, the original books are great to read; as they provide lots of examples. This repetition can help to embed the lessons into your psyche. With that being said, stripping these lessons down to their core substance will help you to focus on the things that really matter. As I'm sure we can agree, time is also very valuable. I am all about maximizing time.

The Mindset Warrior summaries are here to support your journey toward a resilient mindset. **www.mindsetwarrior.com**

Section 1 –
Setting The Stage

Chapter 1 – Getting Started

The basic premise of "Leaders Eat Last" is that a leader that succeeds long term is one that focuses on the people's best interest.

I think the principles inside the book extend beyond organizational leadership. They can be applied to being a good friend, parent, and team member in general.

My biggest criticism is that the book lacked clear actionable advice. It really stayed in the realm of theory and vaguery for the most part. I found that many of the stories or attempts to make connections diluted the impact of certain points. Some of the chapters felt out of order, so in order to compensate for that, I have rearranged the summary in what I view as a more appropriate flow.

After multiple reads, and listening to hours of Simon's lectures, I've translated the theories into application. I've condensed them into 18 principles. Each principle contains an objective, reasons why it matters, and how to implement it.

If you've read some of the reviews on the original book, the consensus is pretty clear that the book could have been a lot shorter. If you've seen Simon's TedX talk or other talks; let alone if you've read any leadership book, you've likely heard of these principles, but oftentimes its the frame that is provided that truly allows the information to be retained. I hesitated to pick up the book for a while due to my underestimation of its added value, but at the end of the day, I'm glad I did. In this summary, I've kept the frame, and removed the fluff. Let's get started.

Chapter 2 – The Biology of Humans

based on ch.5 & 6

OBJECTIVE: Balancing the hormones of the team

The 4 hormones that contribute to feelings of happiness are:

endorphins

dopamine

serotonin

oxytocin

These 4 hormones can be divided into 2 categories:

selfish chemicals

endorphins

dopamine

pro-social chemicals

serotonin

oxytocin

The selfish chemicals motivate us to pursue our own goals. These are often released in times of scarcity.

endorphins = mask physical pain and increase endurance

ex: runner's high

NOTE: laughing increases endorphins

dopamine = incentivizes us to progress

ex: eating, suppressing anxiety through drug use, etc.

It drives us to set goals (*goals must be tangible (specific)*)

NOTE: beware of what behavior you reinforce (more on this in principle 13 on taming dopamine)

serotonin = feelings of pride - "the leadership chemical"

ex: getting a raise, winning a reward, etc.

Raises your status.

Increases accountability to the group.

Getting attention for your behavior increases serotonin.

One of the great features of serotonin is that the more recognition (increased serotonin) we receive, the more apt we are to feel obligated to give back to the group.

oxytocin = love and trust

ex: being a part of a church, helping with hurricane relief, the doctor's office offering free coffee and snacks

It is released when we give and receive time, energy, and resources.

It is also released when we witness (see or hear about) acts of generosity

It is responsible for feelings of empathy.

When we feel safe with a person or place, we are likely experiencing oxytocin.

The more time we spend with someone, the more apt we are to make ourselves vulnerable around them. When we are willing to be vulnerable it sends a message to our subconscious mind that we are safe.

Its important to reduce perceived threats by keeping the flow of communication open. Engaging with people throughout the day helps them avoid feeling like they need to protect themselves. This allows them to extrovert; rather than introvert, their attention

Chapter 3 – Taming Cortisol

based on ch.7

OBJECTIVE: Avoid activating cortisol by increasing feelings of safety

<u>When cortisol is high:</u>

- It incites paranoia and a focus on self preservation. This reduces an individuals ability to contribute productively to the group.

- It is responsible for the fight or flight response when a threat is perceived.

- It increases paranoia; leading us to focus on trying to identify a threat in the environment.

- It inhibits oxytocin *(feelings of empathy)* and increases aggression

- The immune system becomes more vulnerable when cortisol is present

One of your key duties in the workplaceis to reduce cortisol. Many environments outside of the workplace are threatening in and of themselves, its imperative to keep cortisol in check in the workplace for better overall cooperation and performance. One of the big culprits of high cortisol is uncertainty. Focus on increasing certainty in the workplace.

HOW:

- clearly communicate standards

- demonstrate consistent consequences

- have a feedback system that is frequent

- build trust through integrity and interest in the team members overall well being

- have incentive structures that don't impede collaboration

- avoid layoffs as a default

<u>Company Example = Next Jump's "Lifetime Employment Policy"</u>

Next Jump's policy basically states that they will not fire you. This forces the company leaders to be much more strategic with hiring, and it forces them to focus heavily on programs that train and nurture their employees.

Results of its implementation:

- More information sharing and cooperation because team members didn't have to fear for their jobs (aka less cortisol)

- Average revenue growth jumped from 25% to 60% per year

- Increased loyalty: Their turnover rate dropped from 40% *(industry average)* to 1%

NOTE: more importantly than compensation, it seems people prefer safety and belongingness

Chapter 4 – The Societal Shift From Cooperation to Self Interest

based on ch 11 &12

Chapter 11 & 12 provides a history lesson on how society shifted from a "group-focused" mentality to an "individual-focused" one.

The shift from shared hardship and service to our modern excessive consumerism and self focus is said to have started with the baby boomer generation.

Generations prior to the baby boomers heavily emphasized the need to serve others. The baby boomer generation (1946 – 1964) ignited the serving of self.

Initially the contrast and tension in values between the earlier generations that experienced more social reliance, and the later ones that were more individual focused, helped to keep things in balance, but as we move further away from the earlier generations, we've lost sight of our loyalty to the tribe.

As wealth shifted, mentalities shifted:

- economics shifted closer to saving our wealth vs. sharing our wealth

- mentalities shifted from protecting people to protecting commerce

Companies started to demonstrate more concern for self than their employees; easily willing to lay off people who dedicated years to the company. This lack of commitment to the employee's merit and instead a focus on economics, brought distrust (more cortisol) into the workplace.

--- EVENTS DISCUSSED

the great depression

- left nearly 1/4 of the country jobless

- ended 1942

- required loyalty and collaboration

world war 2

- 133 million Americans with 16 million in military
- provided the nation a felt sense of being part of something bigger than self

The baby boomers being raised in the transition from scarcity to a state of more affluence made the contrast very apparent.

This led to a heightened desire to protect this new; more affluent, way of living. The focus on persevering affluence inevitably shifted to more individualism.

NOTE: even political parties became less collaborative and more distant as affluence shifted.

As baby boomers aged, the 1980s highlighted the presence of abundance:

- new economic theories to protect wealth were introduced

- a rise in the disposability of products increased (ex: the disposable camera)

At the core of what is responsible for this sort of dehumanization is abundance. Scale creates distance, and distance results in the abstract value of things. We now have an abundance of what we need and want. This abundance leads to destructiveness. The modern scale that we operate in causes us to lose meaning.

By prioritizing people, we get better results long term.

In order to counteract the focus on individualism in society, be sure to avoid incentivizing selfish behaviors, and in order to avoid the modern day abstraction; due to increases in solely virtual relationships and an abundance of resources, instill practices that keep the team engaged and reliant on each other.

Chapter 5 – Understanding The Leadership Transaction

based on ch.8

OBJECTIVE: Understanding the relationship between a leader and their team.

History has taught us that having an "alpha" lends itself to better cooperation. At the root of leadership is self sacrifice ("leaders eat last")

The perks of leadership are transactional. The leader receives "special treatment" as a reward for their willingness to put themselves at risk. On the other hand the team members experience less responsibility and stress but accept a "lesser treatment". We witness this across a variety of societies and institutions.

EX: celebrities receiving extra service, president getting special seating, etc.

People want to led because they want to support the genes that will protect them when danger is present.

NOTE: Witnessing leaders as a contrasting element drives the motivation to increase status among team members. This is important because due to the fact that status is given socially, the desire to increase status is responsible for keeping people behaving socially responsibly.

NOTE: While material goods can give the illusion of status, true status needs to earned to be felt.

The rank of "leader" develops overtime after being accepted at a higher status as a person continues to display their willingness to sacrifice for the team, and the trust of the team members increases.

Trust = a biological reaction to the belief that someone has your best interest at heart

NOTE: Authority doesn't equate to leadership

The ultimate goal of leadership in an organization is to create a balance between dopamine, endophins, oxytocoin, serotonin. This balance makes up the entirety of this book's message.

Section 2 – The Principles

Principle 1 – The Willingness to Sacrifice

based on ch.1

OBJECTIVE: Find ways to demonstrate the willingness to sacrifice for your team

Leaders willing to sacrifice their time and energy for the group will yield a more loyal group.

HOW:

- Show up early and stay late.

- Periodically involve yourself in the grunt work.

Principle 2 – Equal Treatment

based on ch.2

OBJECTIVE: Demonstrate your commitment to "fairness".

Remove the sense of danger sometimes felt in group situations by increasing feelings of safety within the team.

Be sure to perform in ways that indicate "I am cared for".

REMEMBER:

to earn trust you have to give trust

to earn care you have to give care

If team members see that others have unearned privilege or are granted more trust without any clear reason, it reduces their feelings of being cared for.

HOW:

- Focus on merit based treatment. The goal is to replace obligation with pride.

Principle 3 – A Sense of Belonging

based on ch.3

OBJECTIVE: Ignite the sense of belongingness in team members

The world is full of threats *(more cortisol)*.

In order to elicit the cooperation you desire, the team members must feel like the other people on the team have their best interest in mind.

There are external threats and internal threats. While we can't control outside threats, we can control inside ones.

outside threats =

tech changes

familial changes

internal threats =

feeling dumb

feeling useless

HOW:

- maintain a strong culture

- give people the power to make decisions

- demonstrate a commitment to auditing who comes in

NOTE: Make sure that the leader is responsible for forming the circle of safety, otherwise each individual will try to create a circle of safety for themselves, which often lead to politics *(hiding information)*. As a leader, you often have a better vantage point, and thus are able to make more educated decisions.

Principle 4 – Acknowledgement

based on ch.4

OBJECTIVE: Give regular feedback and acknowledgment.

REMEMBER: Ignoring is worse than criticism. In one study, people who were criticize were found to be more engaged than those who were not.

A sense of control matters. We can increase our team members sense of control by giving acknowledgment.

Effort without acknowledgment increases stress *(more cortisol)*. Increased acknowledgment leads to the perception of increased control.

NOTE: 1 study found that workers stress wasn't caused by more responsibility, but less feelings of control throughout the day.

People who attend work unhappy are actually likely to do things to make others unhappy. ("misery loves company")

NOTE: 1 study found that not having a job is better than having a threatening work environment.

HOW:

- have a system that provides consistent feedback (the book "The 4 Disciplines of Execution" has a great system for this. You can get my summary that outline's their process <u>here</u> > www.

mindsetwarrior.com/summary-guides)

- find ways to reward people for the effort they give

Principle 5 – Give Up Control

based on ch.9

OBJECTIVE: Nurture creative problem solving

By demonstrating your willingness to give up control, you increase the trust in you as a leader and you help improve team members individual competence too. Confidence within a team is often derived from how much we feel trusted by leaders.

Many leaders grasp tightly to control at their organization's expense. In those situations people begin following the rules just to prevent losing their jobs at the expense of actually solving the problem efficiently.

HOW:

- train the team to hold the mindset that rules are for normal operations

- train team members to develop competency and confidence by lending decision authority

Principle 6 – A Cooperative Environment

based on 10

OBJECTIVE: Nurture an environment of cooperation

When a company fails to make progress, it is the environment not the people that are the problem.

the neocortex = gives us the ability to communicate and pass on lessons (logic)

limbic brain = controls feelings, and gives us ability to form emotional bonds (emotion)

Often leaders will focus on logic and skill *(the neocortex)* in the workplace, but even more important is focusing on the emotional bond *(limbic brain)*.

A focus on collaboration over individual intellect produces better results.

Simon gives the example of a snowmobile in the middle of a desert. Yes, it'll likely run, but it won't run as efficiently. Its not the snowmobile that is the issue, its the environment.

Trust in the workplace leads to an environment conducive to performance.

HOW:

- emphasize collaboration in the company culture

- reward behaviors that promote collaboration

- have consequences for behaviors that are anti-collaborative.

Principle 7 – Removing Abstraction

based on ch 13,14, & 15

OBJECTIVE: Decrease abstraction

The further connected we feel from others, the harder it is to empathize and the more capable we become of doing harm.

Numbers are abstract. Instead of focusing on numbers, focus on the people's display of commitment to the group.

Care increase as familiarity increases

With abstraction and distance comes less accountability. In these scenarios it is easy to lose sight of the impact of our behaviors, and way of thinking.

Ex: bullying on social media

HOW:

- encourage intermingling amongst higher status employees with lower status ones

- emphasize the broader mission of the company's impact

- encourage leaders to care more for people than metrics

- understand there is a difference between the right thing and what is legal *(avoid demonstrating to your employees that you're more concerned with exploiting a legal system)*

- use visuals

- have meetings in person versus video conference or teleconference

- show the employees tangible results of their efforts *(in person testimonial)*

- find ways to demonstrate your commitment to giving your time and energy

Principle 8 – A Sense of Pride

based on Ch.17

OBJECTIVE: nurture a culture of pride

Get employees to identify their sense of self with the company culture.

Bad ("selfish") behavior is often a result of what is allowed in an environment, not necessarily a bad person.

HOW:

- empower people to make decisions

- encourage the sharing of ideas and information amongst the team

- maintain a practice of sharing mistakes (vulnerability) among the team.

- avoid setting up a system of simple compliance, but more so of taking responsibility

Principle 9 – Avoid Isolation

based on Ch.18

OBJECTIVE: Nurture a culture of interdependency

When distance is created, trust is reduced. There are many historical accounts where leaders were distant from their team, and it often led to tyranny.

If the team members don't feel responsible for their decisions, engagement will drop. This sort of isolation often leads to people covering up their behaviors in order to preserve their status in the group.

HOW:

- Provide the direction for the groups ambitions, then let the team members figure out how to accomplish it

- Avoid keeping control focused at the top by sharing information regularly

- Focus less attention on the leaders power

- Encourage ownership of behavior by lending decision authority to team members

Principle 10 – Integrity First

based on Ch.19

OBJECTIVE: Promote honesty and responsibility

People are constantly evaluating their environment to determine who they should make themselves vulnerable to. We make this assessment by evaluating what someone says compared to what they do.

Knowing what to expect is the most important ingredient to trust. We're constantly seeking to become more certain *(less cortisol)* about our environment. If integrity is broken, uncertainty sets in *(more cortisol)*.

Team members need to feel that what they are being told is in the best interest of the entire group, not just the leaders.

Losing integrity can be as subtle as asking a team member to tell a white lie.

ex: asking your secretary to tell someone on the phone that you have left for the day when you are actually there and available.

HOW:

- demonstrate the willingness to confess mistakes at the sacrifice of your self image

- make it safe to communicate mistakes and dangerous to hide them

Principle 11 – Creating Camaraderie

based on Ch.20

OBJECTIVE: Promote friendship within the team.

Disconnection from coworkers leads to more concern for self, which often will result in less cooperation.

Getting together out of context helps form trust (ex: company outings)

Commonality is the basis of friendship, so find some way for your team members to see similarities in each other.

HOW:

- promote the sharing of personal information

- add company bonding events

Principle 12 – People Before Numbers

based on Ch.21

OBJECTIVE: Focus more on employees sense of safety over shareholders and metrics

While focusing on numbers will help short term, if you seek to put the culture first, you'll last long term.

Empowerment compared to directiveness leads to better results long term.

Feeling safe and feeling like your leaders have your best interest in mind will yield better work ethic.

If employees do not feel committed to the company, it will show in their interactions with customers, and this in turn will lead to lower profits.

HOW:

- Use layoffs as a last resort.

- Promote internally.

- Avoid removing people based on numbers; instead stick to merit.

Principle 13 – Taming Dopamine

based on Ch.22

OBJECTIVE: Control the dopamine in your environment

Our focus on systems and metrics often gives us an excess reliance on them; leaving us out of touch with each other.

REMEMBER: Dopamine exists to reward behaviors that support life.

The completion of each step closer to a goal *(improvement in metrics)* gives us a hit of dopamine. At the same time, putting the mind at rest through distraction, alcohol, nicotine, and drugs also activate dopamine.

Because of this chemicals nondiscriminatory nature, its important to keep our desire for dopamine hits in check.

HOW:

- Avoid incentive programs that drive dopamine addiction.

- Avoid incentives for individual behaviors that leads to perverse incentives like personal metrics. Consider shifting incentives to group metrics. Doing this rewards cooperation *(more Oxytocin)* compared to individualism.

Principle 14 – Justice

based on Ch.23

OBJECTIVE: Create rules that prevent corruption

If there is no need to rely on others, individuals will look after their own self interest.

Often rules will be bent and broken if there is no one to hold yourself accountable to.

Principle 15 – Focused Connection

based on Ch.24

OBJECTIVE: Create an environment of focus

In describing recent generations, the word "entitlement" gets thrown around a lot. Simon believes what is called entitlement is actually impatience.

This impatience is derived from 2 misunderstandings:

- success isn't instant

- the devaluation of hard work because of ease to access

Easy access make us reliant on dopamine.

BEWARE of distraction

Increases in ADHD diagnosis over the recent decade illustrates an increasing distractability in our society

Technology takes us away from truly mastering presence and connection.

Getting too comfortable with abstraction causes the mind to confuse passive engagement with true commitment.

EX: re-tweeting about a cause can satisfy the human desire for contribution, but an investment of energy and time would have a larger impact

BEWARE of isolation

Primarily due to advances in technology, we are becoming increasing reliant on virtual relationships. Studies have found that feelings of loneliness increase with the more use of social media. The regular use of it also lends itself to unfair comparisons that can affect people's self esteem.

Principle 16 – Service First

based on Ch.25

OBJECTIVE: Create a culture of service

Selflessness breaks dopamine addiction.

NOTE: the completion of the 12 step *(the commitment to help another alcoholics recover)* of alcoholic anonymous has been connected with decreasing the likelihood of relapse.

The addition of another person yields better behavioral cooperation due to the extra accountability.

NOTE: one study found that the presence of oxytocin *(cooperation hormone)* helps fight withdrawal symptoms in heroin addicts and alcoholics. There is also some suggestion that the presence of oxytocin might help prevent dependence to begin with.

HOW:

- reward behaviors of cooperation

- find ways to have team members rely on each other

Principle 17 – Add Hardship

based on Ch.26

OBJECTIVE: increase cooperation through shared struggle

In this chapter, Simon talks about the importance of removing abundance in the work environment.

He says that what is in abundance is often taken for granted and it is perceived as having less value.

He suggests that it is important to feel a shared burden in order to increase the cooperative hormone, oxytocin.

Simply put,

less hardship = less Oxycontin = less cooperation

shared hardship = more Oxycontin = more cooperation

NOTE: Soldiers who deploy commit suicide at a slightly lower rate than those who do not.

RE-Define Struggle

Often small companies are the ones who innovate the most. There is something about limited resources that get people to be more creative.

REMEMBER: growth itself doesn't ignite the mind, there must be some sort of struggle to conquer.

A focus on vision compared to small short term steps ignites better; more engaged, focus.

HOW:

- Periodically look for ways to reasonably exaggerate external threats to the team's success

- Find ways to add pressure with challenge; yet realistic, deadlines

Principle 18 – The Circle of Safety

based on Ch.27

OBJECTIVE: Commit to empathy

Leadership is a commitment to form a circle of safety through empathizing with team members.

Leadership is about demonstrating the willingness to sacrifice the self.

GIVEAWAY

I turned these 18 principles into a 1 page action sheet. Use it as a quick reference to create a strategy around enhancing your personal or company culture, or print it out and post it on your office wall to keep these leadership principles top of mind.

You can **download the PDF here >**

www.mindsetwarrior.com/18-principles

Conclusion

Simon's leadership principles aren't uncommon. In "Leaders Eat Last" he didn't necessarily innovate a radical shift in leadership; instead he provided a framework to remember why certain ways of operating and thinking as a leader matters.

I especially enjoyed his angle of focusing on how certain practices affect our physiologically. "Leaders Eat Last" goes hand in hand with the popular, "How to Win Friends And Influence People" classic (you can checkout my summary on that book > http://mindsetwarrior.com/cs-summaries). In both of these book, the principles are practically the same, but the frame is different. If you're someone *(like myself)* that needs more concrete reasons why you should implement an action or way of thinking, I think "Leaders Eat Last" better serves that end.

As stated in the beginning of this summary, this book could have been a lot shorter, but if you're one who likes and/or needs a lot of extra anecdotes, you might consider reading the full book. Otherwise, I feel very confident that I've provided a succinct clear summary of his leadership principles that doesn't water them down, but also removes the fluff. Keep this summary around, and grab the 18 principles action sheet

(http://mindsetwarrior.com/cs-18-principles) to help you in your implementation.

Here are some quick bookmarks from earlier:

Want a quick refresher on the hormones we must focus on balancing in our tribe? (click here)

Want a refresher on how to remove abstraction in the group? (click here)

Do you remember the transaction you signed up for as a leader? (click here)

REMEMBER don't forget to grab the principles action sheet >

http://mindsetwarrior.com/cs-18-principles

BONUS

Biases cloud our decision making on a day-to-day basis. You may have learned about a few of our cognitive biases back in your college or high school psychology class. It is time we get a refresher and understand how cognitive biases truly color our daily lives.

While we can't completely escape our biases, having an understanding of them can give us an advantage.

Get the FREE Cognitive Bias Report >

http://bit.ly/MWCogBiasReport

Other Mindset Warrior Summaries that might interest you:

Getting to Yes: Negotiating Agreement Without Giving In
(sales & negotiation)

How to Win Friends & Influence People
(relationships)

The 4 Disciplines of Execution: Achieving Your Wildly
Important Goals
(productivity)

Never Split The Difference: Negotiating As If Your Life
Depended On It
(sales & negotiation)

Visit www.mindsetwarrior.com/cs-summaries

FEEDBACK:

If you'd like to provide feedback on how I can better improve these books, your opinion would be very much appreciated. Please send me an email at: summaries@mindsetwarrior.com

I would love to hear from you.

- Alexa Taylor (The Mindset Warrior)

88324108R00033

Made in the USA
Columbia, SC
28 January 2018